Creepy Creatures

Mosquitoes

Sue Barraclough

Raintree

Chicago, Illinois

Printed and bound in China by South China Printing Company Ltd.

09 08 07 06 05
10 9 8 7 6 5 4 3 2 1

Library of Congress Cataloging-in-Publication Data
A copy of the cataloging-in-publication data for this title is on file with the Library of Congress.
  Mosquitoes / Sue Barraclough
  ISBN 1-4109-1507-7 (HC), 1-4109-1512-3 (Pbk.)

Acknowledgments
The publisher would like to thank the following for permission to reproduce copyright material:
Alamy Images pp. 8-9 (22DigiTal), 4 (Fogstock), 7top 7bottom (Holt Studios International Ltd),13 (NaturePicks), 21 (Roger Eritja), 18 (Wildimages); Ardea p. 6 (Steve Hopkin); Bubbles p. 23; Corbis pp.10-11 (CDC/PHIL), 5 (Pat O'Hara); FLPA p.14 (David T. Grewcock); Garden Matters p. 22 (M Collins); Holt Studios International Ltd p.12; NHPA pp. 19, 20 (George Bernard); Science Photo Library pp.17 (Claude Nuridsany & Marie Perennou), 15 (Darwin Dale), 16 (David M.

Cover photograph reproduced with permission of Corbis /CDC/ PHIL

Every effort has been made to contact copyright holders of any material reproduced in this book. Any omissions will be rectified in subsequent printings if notice is given to the publisher.

Some words are shown in bold, **like this**. You can find out what they mean by looking in the glossary on page 24.

Contents

Mosquitoes 4

Types of Mosquitoes 6

Looking for Mosquitoes 8

A Mosquito's Body 10

A Mosquito's Head 12

Mosquito Noises 14

A Mosquito's Eggs 16

Growing and Changing 18

Food for Mosquitoes 20

Dangerous Mosquitoes 22

Glossary 24

Index 24

Mosquitoes

Mosquitoes are tiny flies. Some are so small that they are difficult to see.

You need a magnifying glass to see a mosquito clearly.

5

Types of Mosquitoes

Gnats and midges belong to the same family as mosquitoes.

mosquito

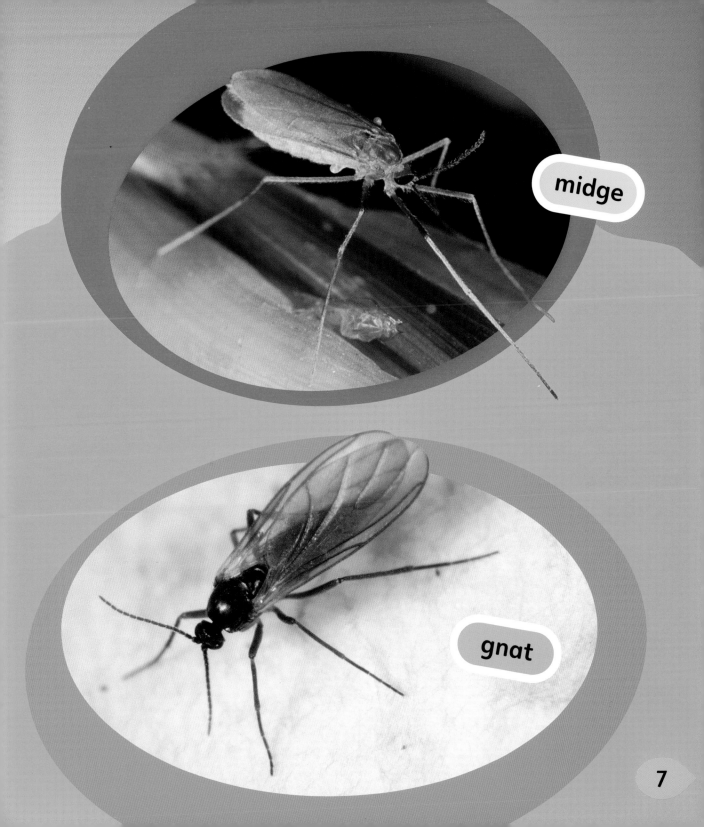

midge

gnat

Looking for Mosquitoes

Mosquitoes live near ponds and ditches.

You might see them on a summer evening.

A Mosquito's Body

Mosquitoes are **insects**. Their bodies have three parts.

thorax

head

They have six long legs.
How many can you count?

abdomen

A Mosquito's Head

A mosquito has very **sharp** mouthparts for piercing and sucking.

Slurp, slurp!

Their feather-like **antennae** are used for touching and smelling.

antennae

Mosquito Noises

Mosquitoes make a whining sound as they fly around.

EEEEEEEEEEEeeeeeeeeeeee!

Zzzzzzzzzzzzz!

Their wings beat so fast that they make this noise.

A Mosquito's Eggs

A **female** mosquito lays hundreds of eggs on still water.

She lays them in groups that f l o a t together.

Growing and Changing

The egg changes
into a **larva**
that **wriggles**
in the water.

Finally, the adult mosquito waits for its wings to dry. Then it can fly away.

Food for Mosquitoes

Male mosquitoes eat **nectar** that they suck from flowers.

Females eat blood that they suck from animals.

Dangerous Mosquitoes

When mosquitoes suck blood from people, they can spread **diseases**.

Ouch!

There are creams
that can help
if you are bitten.

Glossary

antenna (More than one are antennae.)
feeler on an insect's head
that helps it smell, see, or hear

disease sickness

female girl insect

insect animal with three body parts and
six legs

larva (More than one are called larvae.)
first stage of an insect's life when it
eats and grows

male boy insect

nectar sweet liquid in flowers

Index

antennae 13

blood 21

disease 22

eggs 16, 17

larvae 18

mouthparts 12

nectar 20

wings 14, 15, 19

Notes for Adults

The *Creepy Creatures* series supports children's growing knowledge and understanding of their world, introducing them to many smaller insects and animals. When used together, the eight books in the series enable comparison of the similarities and differences between these creepy creatures.

These books also help children extend their vocabulary as they hear new words. Since words are used in context in the book, this should enable young children to gradually incorporate them into their own vocabulary. You may like to introduce and explain some new words in this book such as *thorax, abdomen, mouthparts, antennae, larva, nectar,* and *diseases.*

Additional information
Mosquitoes are small and delicate, but they are one of the most dangerous blood-sucking insects. In some tropical countries, female mosquitoes can spread diseases such as malaria, and they are the cause of millions of deaths every year. Mosquitoes feed mostly at dusk or during the night. Female mosquitoes need a meal of blood because this provides proteins necessary for the development of their eggs. Some mosquito breeding grounds can be treated with insecticides, and draining and filling of ponds and ditches is sometimes carried out as a more permanent solution. However, these methods of control may cause pollution and other environmental damage.

Follow-up activities
• Take children to a nearby pond where they can make their own observations about mosquitoes.
• Talk about what children find interesting about mosquitoes.
• Encourage children to record their ideas and observations in drawings, paintings, or writing.